The Classroom E

MW00906415

Grades 4-7

Written by Heather Cooper
Illustrated by Tom Goldsmith and Tom Riddolls

About the author: Heather Cooper works for the Limestone District School Board and has taught in the primary, junior, and intermediate divisions. She has degrees from Concordia University and Lakehead University. Her mother was in politics.

ISBN 978-1-55035-875-9
Copyright 2008
All Rights Reserved * Printed in Canada

Published in Canada by:
S&S Learning Materials
15 Dairy Avenue
Napanee, Ontario
K7R 1M4
www.sslearning.com

At a Glance

Learning Expectations	What is Government?	Forming Parties	Choosing a Leader	Campaigning	Voting & Citizenship	Mock Parliament	Conclusion & Assessment
Language Skills							
• Reading comprehension	•	•	•	•	•	•	•
• Summarize events/details	•	•	•	•	•	•	•
• Communicate orally	•	•	•	•	•	•	•
• Communicate in writing	•	•	•	•	•	•	•
• Develop vocabulary	•	•	•	•	•	•	•
Reasoning & Critical Thinking Skills							
• Make comparisons	•	•	•	•	•	•	•
• Develop opinions and personal interpretations	•	•	•	•	•	•	•
• Make inferences (e.g., why events occurred)	•		•	•	•	•	
• Develop research skills	•	•		•	•		•
• Analyze and evaluate historical information		•	•	•			•
• Recognize the validity of differing points of view			•	•	•	•	
• Use graphs and diagrams	•	•		•	•	•	•
Understanding							
• Understand elections and why they are held	•		•	•	•	•	•
• Understand how to hold an election			•	•	•		
• Understand how Canada's political system is organized	•	•	•			•	•
• Understand how to campaign for an election				•	•		
• Understand what a platform is		•	•	•			
• Describe the roles and responsibilities of people involved in an election			•	•	•		•
• Analyze, synthesize, and interpret election results					•		
• Understand the history of elections in Canada						•	•
• Understand some of the problems and issues associated with elections		•	•	•	•	•	•

Table of Contents

Introduction

This resource teaches elections and citizenship through experiential learning. The more involved the students become in the activities, the better their understanding of how these processes work in Canada.

The approach also provides numerous ways to assess students on a variety of skills including reading and writing, knowledge of the Canadian Government unit, applying math, critical thinking, oral communication, and interpersonal skills. Students have the opportunity to demonstrate their skills on paper, orally, and through actions. They also have a chance to make many of their own choices thereby increasing accountability. The activities and process outlined is designed to be flexible so that teachers may balance the level of student freedom according to the situation. Students are given the chance to form their own opinion about many issues that face our country today and to discover ways that they can be a part of the process.

The resource is organized in six sections, each with teacher guidelines referring to specific worksheets as well as classroom setup and extension considerations. Student worksheets follow. It is not necessary to do all of the worksheets to have a successful classroom election, but everything you may need to run a complete election is included to ensure your students experience the excitement and hard work of an election firsthand.

Web Sites

The following web sites contain information that may help during the classroom election. They can be used for student research and for teacher information.

http://www.leg.bc.ca/info/bcti/2006/spring/lp3.htm
http://www.educationworld.com
http://en.wikipedia.org
http://www.cbc.ca/
http://www.ndp.ca/
http://www.liberal.ca/default_e.aspx
http://www.greenparty.ca/
http://www.conservative.ca/

Other Resources

Francis, D. *Discovering Canada's Government*. Oxford University Press; Canada, ©2001.
Granfield, L. *Canada Votes. How We Elect Our Government*. Kids Can Press; Toronto, Canada, ©1997.
McTeer, M. *Parliament: Canada's Democracy and How It Works*. Random House of Canada; Canada, ©1995.
Stanbridge, J. *Who Runs This Country, Anyway? A guide to Canadian Government*. Scholastic Canada Ltd.; Toronto, Canada, ©2005.
Wells, D. (editor). *Canadian Unity, Canadian Government*. Weigl Educational Publishers Limited; USA, ©2005.

Time Line Sample

This sample timeline is spread over a three-month period with one period a day (30 min to 1 hour). It includes all activities up to and including the election, but not mock parliament and assessment.

Day	Section	Worksheets	Election Milestones
1	What is Government	KWL Chart, Personal Glossary	
2		Levels of Government	
3		Government Structure	
4		The Federal Government	
5		How Are School and Government Alike?	
6	Forming Parties	Canada's Political Parties	
7		Which Party Do You Agree With?	
8		Your Personal Platform	**Teacher forms parties**
9	Choosing a Leader	Government Leaders	
10		Nominations – What Is a Good Leader? Who Will You Nominate?	
11			**Parties nominate and choose a leader**
12	Campaigning	Election Checklist, Campaign Time	
13		Your Parties Platform, Final Platform	
14		The Media's Influence	
15		Party Roles	**Planners given, begin work on first speech, posters, commercial, etc.**
16			**Work Period for planners**
17		Candidate Interview, What Would You Like to Learn About a Candidate?, Your Party's Interview Questions	
18			**Work period for interviews**
19			**Interviews**
20		Polling	**First poll**
21			**Speeches, second poll**
22		Holding a Debate, Official Debate Guidelines, How a Debate Works	

Time Line Sample

Day	Section	Worksheets	Election Milestones
23		What Would You Debate?	
24			**Work period for commercials**
25-27		Topics for Debate: Social Issues, Education, Environment, Employment, Health care	
29		Topic of Debate: Your School	
30			**Debate, third poll**
31			**Work period**
32	Voting and Citizenship	The Right to Vote and Canadian Citizenship, You Are a Citizen of Your School	
33		Your Rights and Responsibilities As a Canadian, Rights and Responsibilites of All Canadians, Citizenship Certificate	
34		Coordinate Mapping Activity	
35			**Work period**
36		What Happens After the Election?	
37			**Final speeches, final poll**
38		The Campaign Review	**Group and self assessment. Commercials should be shown throughout the campaign. It is also possible for each party to make more than one.**
39			**ELECTION DAY !**

* Teachers may wish to include more work periods for their class if they feel more independent work time is required.

Speech Rubric

Name:_____   Party: _____

	Level 1	Level 2	Level 3	Level 4
Language	Poor use of language, does not convey the message clearly	Uses words that may be unsuited to the topic, audience, or purpose of the speech; word choice lacks originality	Uses appropriate language and word choice	Uses sophisticated and varied language that is suited to the topic and audience; word choice is concise, original, and effective
Organization	A lack of organization makes it difficult to follow the speaker's ideas	Has some inconsistencies in organization and/or a lack of sustained focus throughout the speech with inconsistently used transitions	Clear attempt at organization with a beginning, middle, and end and an attempt to use transitions	Clear, organized speech with engaging introduction, a sequenced body with appropriate transitions, and a convincing conclusion
Delivery	Lack of eye contact, clarity and projection of voice, tone and pace, and/or appropriate gestures make the speech difficult to follow	Inconsistent use of eye contact, clarity and projection of voice, tone and pace, and/or gestures interrupt the flow of the speech	A combination of appropriate eye contact, clarity, and projection of voice, tone and pace, and gestures are used	A combination of appropriate and effective eye contact, clarity and projection of voice, tone and pace, and gestures significantly enhance the speaker's words
Overall Effectiveness	Did not hold the audience's attention effectively	Held the audience's attention with some effectiveness	Effectively held the audience's attention	Held the audience's attention with a high degree of effectiveness

Group Work Rubric

Name:_____   Party: _____

	Level 1	Level 2	Level 3	Level 4
Teamwork	The team member rarely shows team player qualities	The team member sometimes shows team player qualities	The team member consistently shows team player qualities	The team member always shows team player qualities with a high degree of effectiveness
Roles	The team member was not able to assume a variety of roles	The team member assumed a contributing role in the group	The team member was able to assume a variety of roles within the group	The team member was able to assume a variety of roles within the group, including a leadership role
Contribution	The team member contributed few ideas and information to the group	The team member contributed some ideas and information to the group	The team member contributed information and ideas to the group	The team member contributed a great deal of information and ideas to the group
Communication	The team member communicated with little effectiveness with the group	The team member communicated with some effectiveness with the group	The team member communicated with effectiveness with the group	The team member communicated with the group with a high degree of effectiveness

Commercial Rubric

Name:_____   Party: _____

	Level 1	Level 2	Level 3	Level 4
Content	Little important content is included (candidates views, party name, candidates name, etc.)	Some important content is included	Most needed content is included	All necessary content is included with a high degree of effectiveness
Overall Effectiveness	The commercial did not hold the audience's attention and covers little of the party's points	The commercial holds the audience's attention with some degree of effectiveness and conveys some of the party's points	The commercial holds the audience's attention and effectively covers the party's points	The commercial effectively holds the audience's attention and covers the party's points with a high degree of effectiveness

Debate Rubric

Name:_____   Party: _____

	Level 1	Level 2	Level 3	Level 4
Organization	The issues of the debate are organized with little effectiveness	The issues of the debate are organized with some effectiveness	The issues of the debate are organized with effectiveness	The issues of the debate are organized with a high degree of effectiveness
Arguments and Statements	Few or no arguments or statements of opinion are given	Some arguments and statements of opinion are given	Many arguments and statements of opinion are given	A variety of arguments and statements of opinion are given with a high degree of effectiveness
Use of Facts	Few relevant or supporting facts are used	Some relevant or supporting facts are used	Relevant and supporting facts are used effectively	A variety of supporting facts are used with a high degree of effectiveness
Rebuttal	Few effective counter arguments are made	Some effective counter arguments are made	Effective counter arguments are made throughout the debate	A variety of effective counter arguments are made throughout the entire debate
Overall Effectiveness	The audience was rarely convinced	The audience was sometimes convinced	The audience was effectively convinced	The audience was effectively convinced throughout the debate

Poster Rubric

Name:_____   Party: _____

	Level 1	Level 2	Level 3	Level 4
Content	Few of the poster requirements are included	Some of the poster requirements are included	The poster requirements are included with effectiveness	All of the poster requirements are included with a high degree of effectiveness
Overall Effectiveness	The poster rarely attracts the attention of its audience	The poster attracts the attention of its audience with some effectiveness	The poster effectively attracts the attention of its audience	The poster attracts the attention of its audience with a high degree of effectiveness

Essay Rubric

Name:_____   Party: _____

	Level 1	Level 2	Level 3	Level 4
Language	Little sentence variety and use of unit vocabulary	Some sentence variety and use of unit vocabulary	Effective use of a variety of sentence types and use of unit vocabulary	A variety of sentence types and unit vocabulary are used with a high degree of effectiveness
Content	Few points relate to the assigned topic	Some points relate to the assigned topic	The points stated in the essay effectively relate to the assigned topic	The points stated in the essay relate to the assigned topic with a high degree of effectiveness
Organization	No clear introduction, body, or conclusion	Some organization of paragraphs into an introduction, body, and conclusion	Paragraphs are effectively organized, including an introduction, body, and conclusion	Paragraphs are organized with a high degree of effectiveness, including an introduction, body, and conclusion
Spelling, Conventions, and Grammar	Many, frequent errors are found in the essay	Some errors are found in the essay	Few errors are found in the essay	Little to no errors are found in the essay

Self-Assessment Rubric

Name:_____   Party: _____

	Leve 1	Level 2	Level 3	Level 4
Involvement	I was rarely involved in my party's activities	I was sometimes involved in my party's activities	I was usually involved in my party's activities	I was always involved in my party's activities and often took a leadership role
Teamwork	I rarely contributed ideas and rarely supported others' ideas	I sometimes contributed ideas and sometimes supported others' ideas	I often contributed ideas and usually supported others' ideas	I always contributed ideas and always supported others' ideas
Individual Tasks	I rarely completed my own tasks within the group	I sometimes completed my own tasks within the group	I consistently completed my own tasks within the group	I always completed my own tasks within the group and sometimes helped others with their tasks
Group Role	I took on one role within the group	I sometimes was able to play more than one role within the group	I was able to be a group member as well as a leader	I often took on a leadership role but was able to let others lead as well

Glossary

Bill – The draft version of a law presented in the House of Commons

Cabinet Minister – A minister chosen by the Prime Minister to be responsible for a specific area of the government; for example, the Minister of the Environment

Campaign – The period of time before an election begins when candidates share their views

Candidate – An individual running or competing for an elected position

Caucus – All the Members of Parliament from a political party

Constituency – A district that is able to elect a Member of Parliament

Governor General – The representative of the monarchy in Canada

House of Commons – One of the houses of parliament

Leader of the Opposition – The leader of the party with the second highest number of seats in the house

Majority Government – When the winning party has more than half the seats in parliament

Member of Parliament – An individual elected to serve in the federal parliament

Minority Government – When the winning party has fewer than half the seats in parliament

Party – A group of people sharing similar political views

Platform – The policies that a political party supports

Policy – The plan of action of a person or group

Poll – A preliminary survey to help determine what people think about the candidates and parties

Polling Station – The location where people go to vote

Prime Minister – The leader of the party which has the most seats in the House of Commons

Riding – A district that elects a Member of Parliament (see constituency)

Scrutineer – An appointed party supporter who observes the proceedings at a polling station on Election Day

What is Government?

Goal: This section describes what Canada's government does, who is responsible at different levels of government and how government compares to other aspects of students' lives (e.g., school).

KWL Chart: *(page 15)*
It is important to explore what students already know about the levels of Government in Canada. Have them brainstorm on their own or in a small group to recall what they already know. You may wish to ask students questions as prompts, such as:

When you hear the word government or elections, what do you think of?

Have you heard your family discuss the government at home, especially during an election? What have you heard them say?

What do you know happens during an election?

Once the students have had time to explore on their own, the class should discuss what they already know as a large group. They should then fill out the section about what they want to know. Some questions that can be used as prompts include:

Have you ever wondered how the government affects you as an individual?

Have you wondered who can be involved with the government or how someone becomes involved?

Personal Glossary: *(page 16)*
Students are to use this glossary page to write down new terms and their definitions throughout the unit. Each student may need more than one page. If students are encouraged to write down definitions in their own words, they will have a clear understanding of each term.

Levels of Government: *(page 17)*
The terms on this page should be discussed as a class. The teacher should lead a discussion on the three levels of government and their basic responsibilities. Review the terms municipal, provincial, and federal.
Students are to list all of the different positions at school (e.g., teacher, student, principal, secretary, caretaker, educational assistants, and any other positions that may be at their school).
Students are to compare these positions to how they believe the government works. You may wish to prompt them with questions such as:

Who is responsible for the whole school?

What jobs are the individual people responsible for?

Extension: Students may use the library or Internet to further explore what each level of government does in Canada. Some of the resources named at the front of this book will be of use.

Government Structure: *(page 18)*
Students will research who their political leaders are in their community, province, and country. Students can conduct their research in one of two ways: by asking individuals in the school or at home, or by using the Internet. By typing in the position and the municipality, province or country, they will be able to locate the needed information. The teacher may choose one of these methods or may choose to use a combination of both. This can also be used as a homework assignment.

The Federal Government: *(page 19)*
This can be used as a guided or shared reading lesson. As a class, students can discuss who is currently in each position in Canada. This could also be done as a research activity.

The Federal Government Continued: *(page 20)*
Using chart paper or the chalkboard, the teacher can use this sheet to initiate a brainstorming session with the class. The teacher may prompt the class with questions such as:

Can you think of a law that you need to follow? At school or outside?
How are these laws enforced?

How Are School and Government Alike?: *(page 21)*
Students are to fill out the chart with similarities and differences between their school and the government. The teacher may wish to review the work that was done on levels of government and the previous lesson on laws in Canada.
Students continue by taking three of the points that they brainstormed and explaining why they help both the school and the government run smoothly.

★★   It is important that each of these pages are not only discussed as a class but also taken up as a class. Some students may have more difficulty understanding all of the concepts and taking the pages up will ensure that all students have some understanding. The chalkboard, chart paper, or overhead can be used to show the answers.

Extension:
Find a newspaper article that relates to the Canadian Government and summarize it. Include the following:

The title of the newspaper
Date
The title of the article on the page
The name of the writer
A brief summary of the article

Encourage students to write a letter to someone who currently holds a government position to ask any questions they may have.

KWL CHART

What do you know about elections in Canada?	What do you want to know about elections in Canada?	What have you learned about elections in Canada?

PERSONAL ELECTIONS GLOSSARY

Collect words about Canadian government as you learn them. Record the word in the left column and its definition in the right column.

Word	Definition

LEVELS OF GOVERNMENT

Municipal Government – the level of government that is responsible for a municipality (e.g., cities and towns)

    The *Mayor* is the leader of a municipal government.

Provincial and Territorial Government – the level of government that is responsible for the provinces or territories

    The *Premier* is the leader of the provincial government.

Federal Government – the level of government that is responsible for the country

    The *Prime Minister* is the leader of the federal government.

Make a list of all of the positions of the people at your school (e.g., student, principal).

_____

_____

_____

_____

How are these people and these positions like a government?

_____

_____

_____

_____

What is your role in your school's system? How would that compare to government?

_____

_____

_____

_____

_____

What Is Government?

Name:_____

GOVERNMENT STRUCTURE

Fill out the following chart using the Internet or knowledgeable people at school or at home to show who is in each position and what responsibilities they cover. If you use the Internet you need to type in the position and the specific location (e.g., Mayor Kingston Ontario) into a search engine.

Level of Government	Municipal Government	Provincial Government	Federal Government
Leader	Mayor/Reeve Name:	Premier Name:	Prime Minister Name:
Elected person in your area	Councillor Name:	Member of Provincial Parliament (MPP) Name:	Member of Parliament Name:
Other examples of elected persons	Councillor Name:	MPP Name:	MP Name:
Responsibilities of the level of Government	• Fire protection • Public libraries • Snow removal • Transportation • Waste removal • • •	• Schools • Hospitals • Build roads and highways • Driver's licenses • • •	• Armed forces • Environment • Immigration • • • •

THE FEDERAL GOVERNMENT

The Federal Government is made up of a variety of roles and positions. They include the Prime Minister and the Members of Parliament and some positions that are appointed by the Prime Minister called the Senate.

Because the Government is responsible for making laws, there is also a Judicial Branch that is part of the Government.

The boxes represent all of Parliament. The ovals represent the Judicial Branch of the Government. They are responsible for enforcing the laws and rules made by the government.

Do you know who is currently in each role? Discuss this with your friends and family. You may also use the Internet to help you.

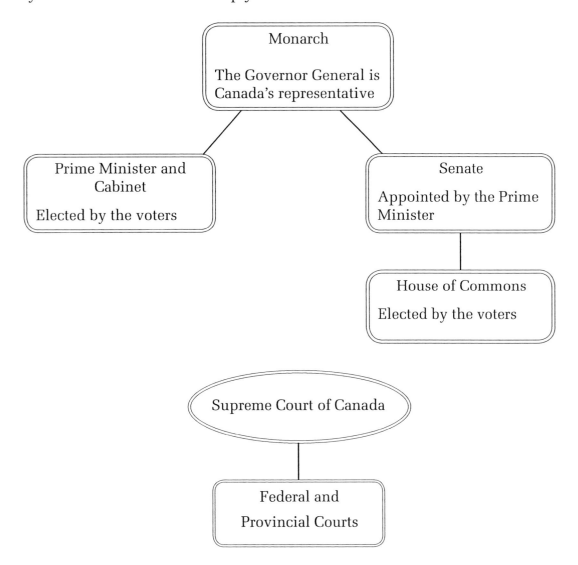

THE FEDERAL GOVERNMENT

The federal government is responsible for making laws for our country.
They are also responsible for ensuring that the laws are followed.

1. Why is it important that our country has laws?

_____

_____

_____

2. What might happen if we did not have laws?

_____

_____

_____

3. What sort of rules or laws does your school have?

_____

_____

_____

4. Why is it important to have rules at school?

_____

_____

_____

5. What might happen to the school, teachers, or students if there were no rules?

_____

_____

_____

_____

HOW ARE SCHOOL AND GOVERNMENT ALIKE?

In the chart below, state ways in which your school and your government are alike. How do these characteristics help things run smoothly? Then list three ways that these similarities help your school and your government run. Be sure to explain how they help.

Similarities	Differences

1. _____

   _____

   _____

2. _____

   _____

   _____

3. _____

   _____

   _____

Forming Parties

Goal: Encourage your students to think about what is important to them and if they were a member of a party, which party it would be.

It is recommended that the class be divided up into parties after these activities have been completed.

Canada's Political Parties: *(page 24)*
To give each student an introductory idea of what each political party believes, read this information as a class.

The teacher should collect a variety of pamphlets, books, and newspaper articles that help explain each party. Pamphlets can be obtained by contacting parties via their web sites or contacting party offices if convenient. It is worthwhile to tell them it is for a particular grade as they may have information that is specific for that age group.

Students should choose three of the political parties and read information from the pamphlets and articles (the Internet may also be used to research the parties). They are to choose a specific belief from each of the three parties and state whether they agree or disagree with their belief.

Which Party Do You Agree With?: *(page 25)*
This exercise is to encourage the students to think about what is important to them. Each student is to complete their own worksheet independently in order to become more familiar with their own beliefs. Teacher prompts may include:
   Was there a particular topic that you felt strongly about?
   Are there big changes that you believe need to be made?
   Are there changes around the school that you think need to be made?

Your Personal Platform: *(page 26)*
Students take issues they have brainstormed and expand on their ideas, mimicking the thinking process members of a political party go through.
   Why do you think this is important?
   Do you believe that others also find it important?
   How do you know? How can you find out?

Dividing the Class into Parties:

The class must be divided up into different political parties for an election to take place. This should be done at the completion of this section. The division can be accomplished in a number of ways. Class size, student involvement, and the teacher's personal preference are factors that may dictate the best scenario for your classroom election.

Scenario #1:

The main political parties in the class's riding can be used to divide up the class. For example, if the parties in your riding are the Progressive Conservatives, the Liberals, the New Democratic Party, and the Green Party, you may choose to divide your class into those four parties. It is important to consider the number of students you put in each party. You may wish to have the numbers in the class represent the approximate ratio of the party representation in parliament. Or you may choose to divide students between parties equally.

Scenario #2:

Given time to research the different existing political parties, students can determine which party they feel they relate to and decide for themselves which party they would like to be in. This gives students a chance to learn about their views and helps them form opinions about what they believe, and act on them. In order to avoid students joining the party to which their friends have chosen, you can have the choice be made anonymously. Be aware that it is unlikely that the resulting parties will be split evenly and some parties may not even be represented at all.

Scenario #3:

The class may form their own parties that do not already exist. Students can determine what they feel is important and build their own platform and title. This allows students to be a part of a party where they have had significant involvement in determining what issues are most important to them, as well as formulating these ideas into a platform. This scenario can work particularly well if the teacher wishes to use school or classroom issues rather than "real" government issues as the basis for the election.

CANADA'S POLITICAL PARTIES

Canada has many federal political parties. The most prominent parties are The Conservative Party, The Liberal Party, The New Democratic Party, and the Bloc Quebecois. The Green Party is also becoming much better known in Canada as well because of the current interest in the environment. These are the parties that compete against each other each election. There are other smaller parties as well.

The Conservative Party: This party is one of Canada's dominating parties. In 2003 the Conservative Party became a combination of the Progressive Conservative Party and the Canadian Alliance Party. A major focus of the Conservative Party is to foster economic growth in the country through private enterprise or individual effort. They have a strong focus on family and family values. Their social views vary greatly.

The Liberal Party: This party seeks a balance between private enterprise and government intervention. They believe that the government should become involved economically where it deems necessary. This party's social views also vary greatly within the party.

The New Democratic Party (NDP): This party believes in the equal distribution of wealth. They are more concerned with equal division than personal economic growth. They believe in economic equality through out the country.

The Bloc Quebecois: This party only has candidates in Quebec, unlike any other federal party. They are the most politically successful separatist party in Quebec history. They believe that because Quebec is very culturally different than the rest of the country they should be their own nation.

The Green Party: This party believes that the environment is the most important issue in the country and world today. They believe that in order to have economic sustainability the environment must first be cared for.

WHICH PARTY DO YOU AGREE WITH?

For three of the parties, using the materials your teacher provides, find an idea, concern, or opinion that they believe is important and state whether you agree or disagree with their statement. Be sure to explain why you have the opinion you do.

1. Party:_____

   Their belief:_____

   _____

   Agree or Disagree? _____

   Your opinion: _____

   _____

2. Party:_____

   Their belief:_____

   _____

   Agree or Disagree? _____

   Your opinion: _____

   _____

3. Party:_____

   Their belief:_____

   _____

   Agree or Disagree? _____

   Your opinion: _____

   _____

Forming
Parties

YOUR PERSONAL PLATFORM

A party's platform is the policy proposals that a party believes in. Parties develop their platform during their election campaign to let voters know what they believe the important issues are.

Create your own personal platform!

1. Think about what you've read and what the different parties believe. What were some specific points that you strongly believe?

2. Do some brainstorming using this graphic organizer. At the end of each arrow, write something that you believe is important (e.g., health care, environment, education).

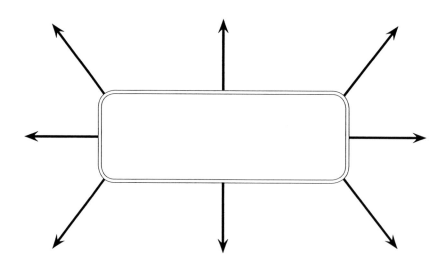

3. Based on the issues you decided are most important, create a name for your personal party. Write the name of your party in the box in the centre.

4. Choose three of the areas you decided are most important. Decide what you would do if you became elected to improve these issues.

_____

_____

_____

_____

Choosing a Leader

Goal: Students will learn about leadership qualities and how they are extremely important when choosing a Canadian government leader.

What Is a Good Leader?: *(page 28)*
Read over the first paragraph on this page as a class. Using the chalkboard or a piece of chart paper brainstorm different leadership qualities. Read over the paragraphs about specific leaders and pull out points and qualities that these strong leaders possess using prompts such as:

What did Agnes MacPhail accomplish?
What qualities did she need to have in order to make this happen?
What did Sir John A. Macdonald accomplish?
What qualities did he need to have in order to make this happen?

Extension: Have students research other famous Canadians and determine what qualities they have that has made them a good leader (e.g., Terry Fox).

Who Will You Nominate in Your Party?: *(page 29)*
Use this worksheet to assist students to generate nominations for leaders of your classroom parties. Encourage students to complete the worksheet independently so that they are not influenced by others and feel free to write their true opinions.

Once students have completed the worksheets they should have a good understanding of who they believe would make a strong leader. Each party is to go through the following steps to determine their leader. Ask students to get into their parties and read out the steps. Each party should do the step as it is read. Give time between each step to ensure decisions can be made. You may want to wander around the room to ensure students are staying on track. Use slips of paper for voting.

1. Anyone in the party may nominate a candidate (they put a person's name forward).

2. Someone in the group must second this motion (agree that this person would make a strong leader).

3. Once there are at least two names put forward, each party determines their leader. All members of the party are to write down one name of the person they believe should be their party leader.

4. The teacher is to count out the votes for each party and they announce the leaders.

WHAT IS A GOOD LEADER?

What do you think makes a strong leader? Although not all leaders are the same, there is a strong chance that many share certain leadership qualities. Think about the following Canadian leaders and what qualities they possessed that made them strong leaders.

Agnes Macphail (1890-1954)

Agnes Macphail began her career as a school teacher before she became involved in politics. When elected in 1921, she was the first woman to become a Member of Parliament. As the only woman, she found her job extremely difficult. Even though she experienced many challenges she persisted and remained an MP for 19 years. Women and groups that needed help were her primary focus. She helped defend those who had trouble defending themselves. She did not leave politics until her poor health stopped her from continuing.

Sir John A. Macdonald (1815-1891)

The first Prime Minister of Canada was Sir John A. Macdonald. Macdonald began his career as a lawyer but he was most been passionate about politics. He was the person that convinced four separate colonies to join together and become the country of Canada. Others had this idea but Sir John A. Macdonald was the one who persisted to make it happen in 1867.

Choose another leader and determine what qualities they have that make them a strong leader. Write their name in the centre circle and their characteristics in the surrounding spaces. What qualities do they have in common with other leaders, including the ones above?

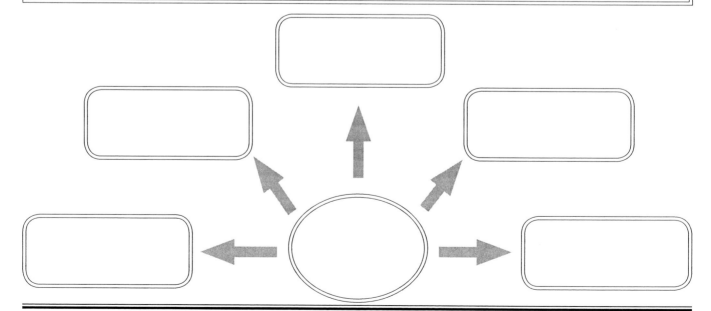

WHO WILL YOU NOMINATE IN YOUR PARTY?

Previously you decided upon qualities that strong Canadian leaders possess. Review these to understand the qualities that strong leaders have and what you believe is important.

What qualities do you believe are important for a leader? Why?

_____

_____

Is there someone in your party that you believe possesses these qualities?

_____

Give examples of how they have demonstrated these qualities.

_____

_____

_____

_____

Who do you think would make a strong political leader in your party?

_____

Why do you believe they are the best candidate?

_____

_____

_____

I nominate _____ **to be leader of our party.**

Campaigning

Goal: Students will appreciate the complexity of a campaign and what a party needs to do in order to be successful. Students will develop a wide range of practical skills in the process.

For the campaign, students are assigned individual roles within the party. There is considerable independent work time in the campaigning of a classroom election, as well as group work. Some students may be able to keep themselves very busy through the entire campaign while others may find their jobs take less time. If you find there are students who finish up their own tasks quickly, they may do any of the following:

1. Assist another group member with their task.
2. Work on an independent research project (page 90).
3. Work on any of the extension activities listed in the teacher notes.

Election Checklist: *(page 37)*
This page should be handed out to each student at the beginning of the campaign to help them keep track of the classroom election. They may check off the items as they are completed to ensure that their party is on track. After each item has been completed, determine what went well about that particular step and what could be improved upon. How could it be improved?

Campaign Time: *(page 39)*
This page is to help students and their parties think about what kind of party they would like to be and how they would like to be perceived.

Read over the page as a group and then have the students read it on their own and answer the questions independently. The questions should be answered on a separate piece of paper and students should be encouraged to answer each question with detail and explain why.

Your Party's Platform: *(page 40)*
Review the concept of a platform and have the students review the sheet they worked on to determine what they felt was important as an individual.

Each party should come up with three platform ideas for each of the following levels: school, community, and country.

If there are members of the party that have similar ideas then these are the ones that they should consider using for their party's platform. If there is a discrepancy as to what issues are important it is the leader's job to make any final decisions.

If the students' parties have been determined for them, they should choose items from an already existing platform which can be located by contacting party offices or found on their web sites.

Extension:

1. Consensus:

   What does consensus mean?

   Did your party come to a consensus easily?

   How did your leader help the party to finally decide?

   What leadership qualities could help a group come to consensus?

Final Platform: *(page 40)*

Once the party has agreed upon their platform ideas they are to write out a good copy to put up in the classroom. This will allow students to review all the parties' platforms throughout the campaign.

Extension: Compare each of the parties' platforms. Use a chart or table to show what is different and what is similar about them.

The Media's Influence: *(page 41)*

The object of this exercise is to help students understand how the media can influence how people perceive politicians and political parties. The teacher may need to ask students in advance to bring in newspapers from home or they may wish to bring in many different newspapers that have been collected over a period of time.

Students should decide if the newspaper article is favourable to a candidate or party or if it could discourage voters from liking them.

Extension: Compare two articles about politicians or political parties and determine what is similar and what is different. Does one article make you like one leader more than another? Why?

Choosing Party Roles: *(page 42)*

The class should discuss all of the roles that are involved in the election. Review the sheet as a large group and then divide up into the separate parties. Each party member should think about which position they might be interested in taking on, and communicate that in discussion with their party members. It is ultimately up to the leader which student takes on which role. Have students review the list of roles on the handout and discuss as a party what they think their strengths and interests are. After the discussion it is the party leader's job to assign roles. Teachers need to ensure that they are monitoring and managing student discussions at this time.

If you have a large class you may find there are not enough roles. Students may double up on roles or you may wish to have them come up with new roles of their own.

Planners for Different Party Roles: *(pages 43-48)*
Planners should be given out after the roles have been decided. The teacher may want to meet with each group to review the roles and ensure that each student is on task.

Campaign Manager – makes sure that the other members of the party are on task. They may also wish to help any party member who is in the greatest in need of assistance at that time.

Speech Writer – needs to meet with the party leader to ensure the correct ideas are being conveyed. The teacher must set speech dates for the students. There should be a minimum of two speeches, one where the candidate introduces their platform and themselves and one right before the election to ensure they have a chance to persuade voters. The teacher should determine a set length of time for each speech. It is recommended that speeches be between two and five minutes.

Commercial Designer – The teacher will need to determine a due date for the commercial. The teacher may also want to use a video camera to tape the commercials and show them as they would be seen on TV.

The teacher may wish to tape a real campaign ad while there is an election going on to give the class some ideas.

Blank Planner – this can be used for any alternate position that the teacher decides upon. Other tasks include poster development and production, interviews of candidates, and polling. Possible roles include art director, reporter, poll manager, cameraman, and scrutineers.

Chief Electoral Officer – The role of the Chief Electoral Officer should be discussed as a class. If there is a student who is a strong independent worker, this is a good role for them. It is also a role that the teacher may wish to discuss but not use in the classroom election. The CEO is in charge of coordinating all aspects of the election. Each party could be given a set amount of supplies and the CEO should ensure that parties are not using more than what is allotted. The CEO can also work with the teacher and class to determine what the class feels are fair rules for their election and to ensure that all parties are remaining positive and not slanderous. It is hard to follow specific election rules because it is different in a classroom but a teacher may spend a period of the class discussing what they believe will make the election fair.
The Chief Electoral Officer may wish to meet with each party to ensure that they are running their campaign honestly, on time, and following all of the rules.

Example classroom election rules:
1. All advertising, speeches, and debates must refrain from being slanderous.
2. Parties should focus on why they should win and not why other parties are "no good".
3. Parties must use only the supplies provided and not exceed their budget.

Accountant – this planner will not take the length of the campaign so another role should be given as well. For example, the accountant could also be responsible for polling, reporting, and interpreting polling results.

Campaign Poster: *(page 49)*
The teacher should review why a poster is so important during a campaign. It may be the first thing that voters see. It also needs to make a positive impression.

Students should be working on the posters throughout the campaign. This is a good job for those who finish their own tasks or who are doubled up with others.

Students should plan out their posters before they begin to make them. The party leader should approve them and may wish to help with the design. Other considerations include where the posters will go. Will they change during the campaign? Who will produce them and put them up (and take them down again)?

Posters can be designed on the computer or by hand.

The teacher will need to plan where posters can be put up, and provide necessary materials for poster creation.

Candidate Interview: *(pages 50-51)*
The class should read over this page beforehand so they can brainstorm more ideas about what they are interested in learning about each candidate.

Each class member is to choose a candidate and list four specific points they would like to find out about that candidate. Once they have their ideas students are to turn these into questions using the blanks at the bottom of the page.

Your Party's Interview Questions: *(page 52)*
Once every class member has completed their own candidate interview questions, they are to get together to come up with a final list of six questions. Again, the leader is responsible for helping the group come to consensus.

Parties must also help prepare their candidate for their interview. They are to review possible topics and what the candidate's answers might be.

One person is selected from each party (any party member other than the party leader) and they will be chosen to ask questions of another party leader in an interview in front of the class.

Extension: Write a brief news report of the interviews. Highlight items candidates discussed well and improvements that could have been made.

 Campaigning

Polling: *(page 53)*
The teacher needs to choose times to hold polls throughout the campaign process. The best times to hold the polls are after a major event (e.g., a speech or debate). There should be at least two speeches, one to state why each candidate/party is the strongest at the beginning, and one before the election to state again why their party should win and what the students will get from that person/party being elected.

Each student in the class needs to be reminded that they are temporarily not a member of a specific political party and that they are to vote as if they were not working with a specific candidate.
To hold a poll, have the students write down the name of the candidate and party they feel would make the best government at this point in the campaign, using a slip of paper for each student. It is the teacher's responsibility to count the votes and inform the class of which party is in the lead. It is important to stress that this is just a poll and not the final vote. It is also important to stress that it is not just the candidate that is being voted on, but the whole party.

Holding a Debate: *(page 54)*
Students are to use this page to determine what they believe is important during a debate. Teachers may want to use a video of a debate, which can be found at most teacher resource libraries. Teachers can also prompt their class by asking the following questions:
- If people have opposing points of view, how could this affect the debate?
- What do you always need to remember when speaking to others?
- How will you make sure that your point comes across clearly?

Students are to use the graphic organizer to brainstorm points of importance and they are to use those points to make final debate guidelines.

The class should share all of the points that they believe are important.

Official Debate Guidelines: *(page 55)*
The teacher should review these guidelines with their class to ensure that everyone knows what is expected. These rules could be posted in the class as a reminder.

How a Debate Works: *(page 56)*
The teacher should review this sheet with the class to ensure their understanding of the steps that are taken in a debate.

Examples of debate topics are provided, but the teacher may also want to brainstorm other topics to help the students think of an idea that interests them.

What Would You Debate? *(page 57)*
All students should participate in this section. Each student should use the debate worksheet to come up with a strong debate of their own. They may choose any topic that interests them to help them understand how a debate works.

© S&S Learning Materials
SSJ1-63 The Classroom Election

It is important to stress that both pros and cons for their topic need to be well prepared.

Classroom Election Debate: *(page 58)*
The teacher may choose to have the entire class fill out this worksheet or they may choose to have only the candidates and/or speech writers do this step.

For the candidate's debate, the candidate and speech writer may choose to work together. The teacher will decide upon the debate topic and the date of the debate. The teacher will need to set a date for the debate to give sufficient time for all candidates to be properly prepared.

The teacher may choose to make the debate topics specifically about the school or they may wish to take on more global issues, such as the environment.

It is often a good time to hold a poll right after a debate.

Topics for Debate: *(pages 59-63)*
The teacher should review these topics with the class. The teacher may want to take a jigsaw approach and have a group of students work on each topic and then present it to the class. Students can find information about each of these topics on the Internet, on party web sites, or in party pamphlets.

Once the students become more familiar with each topic the teacher may choose to use these as debate topics to encourage students to explore the topics further.

Topics For Debate - Your School: *(page 64)*
This sheet is to help students think about possible changes that could be made around their school. After this sheet is completed the teacher may wish to use some of these topics in the official debate.

Classroom Set Up for Debates:

During the debate, the classroom should be set up so that the party leaders are sitting at the front of the room with the rest of the class facing them to act as the audience. You may also wish to have a referee for the debate to ensure that time is distributed fairly and the guidelines for the debate are being followed. The referee should be sitting facing the candidates with his or her back to the audience. They should be located in the middle at the front.

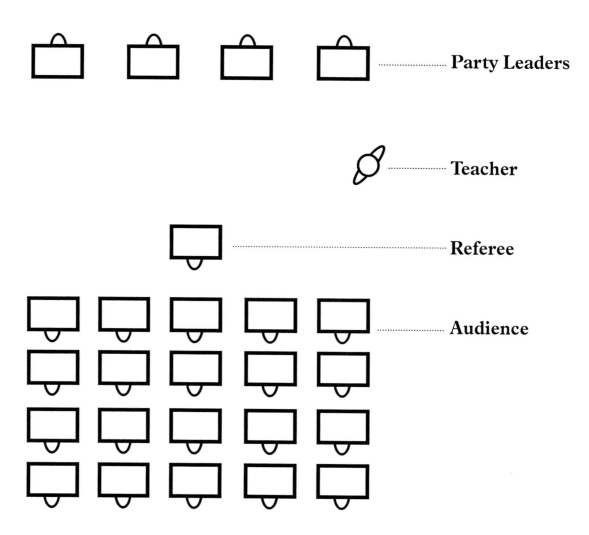

.... **Party Leaders**

.... Teacher

.... **Referee**

.... **Audience**

 Campaigning

Name:_____

ELECTION CHECKLIST

Many steps take place to ensure an election is successful. A process must be followed to make sure all parties are on even ground. Use this checklist to make sure that your party is on track. As you complete a task, check it off to ensure that nothing is missed.

✓	Task	Due Date
	Nominate party leader	
	Choose roles of all party members	
	Plan election budget	
	Party platform preparation	
	Speech preparation	
	Debate preparation	
	Commercial preparation	
	Posters and advertisements	
	Preparation for candidate interview	
	If the successful candidate, the address to the class	

CHOOSING PARTY ROLES

Campaign Manager – The person who oversees the details of a campaign and a candidate's election plan.

Who in your party is organized, pays attention to detail, and is good at leading a group of people? _____

Speech Writer – the individual who writes the speeches for the candidate based on the candidate's campaign.

Who in your party is good with words and language? _____

Head of Advertising – this is the individual who is in charge of the commercials, posters, and advertisements for the candidate.

Who in your party is creative and artistic? _____

Accountant – the individual who is in charge of the budget for an election.

Who in your party is good at math? _____

Chief Electoral Officer – the individual who is a government official and is in charge of co-coordinating all aspects of an election.

Who in your party is very honest and observant? _____

Constituents – the people who vote in a specific area (voting areas are called ridings)

Other roles: (your teacher may assign other roles in addition to the above)

Role:_____ Name:_____

Description:_____

Role:_____ Name:_____

Description:_____

Role:_____ Name:_____

Description:_____

CAMPAIGN TIME

Campaign – the period of time before an election when a party makes their views known. Now that your party has been formed, it is important to start thinking about how you want to go about making your opinions known. You must think about the information that you want to communicate to your voters as well as HOW you would like to communicate this information.

Think about life at your school. What is important to you? Do you see areas that need improvement? What about in your community, province, or country?

Also consider how you would like your party's leader to come across. Do you want to be thought of as kind? Or perhaps tough?

Read the following paragraph and think about what are strengths of the campaign described and what are weaknesses.

Mrs. Jane Roberts is running for Mayor of her city, Salmonville. It is her opportunity to give a speech to her constituency and let them know what she stands for. She begins by explaining why her opponent is not a strong leader and why he would not make a strong Mayor for Salmonville. She then states the main points from her platform. They are as follows:

- The city's recycling program will be stopped because it is a huge expense to the city and there is plenty of room in the landfill for more garbage.

- A new community centre will be built to allow for larger events and better sporting facilities. Some of the money budgeted for this will come from the money that was saved from recycling.

- The six story building limit will be lifted to allow for larger apartment complexes in the centre of the city.

What are the strengths and weaknesses of Mrs. Jane Roberts's ideas?

_____

_____

What are the strengths and weaknesses of her approach?

_____

_____

YOUR PARTY'S PLATFORM

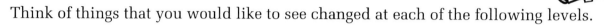

In order to begin your campaign, your party will need to decide what its views are and what they believe is important.

Important: If you are a member of an existing party with a known platform, you should use their opinions from the Internet or pamphlets you've read, as well as your own.

Think of things that you would like to see changed at each of the following levels.

School – an example might be you would like to see new hot lunch items or more daily physical activity time. What other ideas do you have?

1. _____

2. _____

3. _____

Community – an example might be a new community centre with more advanced facilities. What other ideas do you have?

1. _____

2. _____

3. _____

Country – an example might be better health care. What other ideas do you have about what is important to the country?

1. _____

2. _____

3. _____

Name:_____

FINAL PLATFORM

1. Discuss with your party members your ideas for changes.

2. Your party leader should decide which ideas are most popular, and best to use in the party's final platform.

3. The Campaign Manager should choose a party member to write the good copy of the party's final platform to be posted in the classroom to help your voters understand what your party stands for.

The _____ Party's Platform

_____

_____

_____

_____

_____

_____

_____

_____

_____

_____

THE MEDIA'S INFLUENCE

1. Find a newspaper article on a political leader or party that states an opinion.

2. Read the article closely and answer the following:

What is the main idea of this article?

_____

_____

_____

_____

Do you agree with the party or party leader? Why?

_____

_____

_____

_____

Do you believe that the party or party leader would approve of this article? Why or why not?

_____

_____

_____

_____

If you were the journalist, how might you change the article?

_____

_____

_____

_____

Take what you've learned from this article and think about how you would like your leader and your party to be perceived by the media!

Name:_____

CAMPAIGN MANAGER PLANNER

The Campaign Manager plays a very important role during an election. They look after all the details of the election campaign, making sure things are running smoothly and being done on time. It is important that as a Campaign Manager you are organized and good at leading a team of people.

During this election, it is your job to make sure that all of the following is being done and being done on time. You are not responsible for completing the tasks but it is your job to ensure the right person gets it done and that you get them any help they need. Use the blank rows to add other tasks that need to be done.

Task	Due Date	How you will make sure it is complete
Speech Writing		
Posters Displayed		
Debate Preparation		
Commercial Preparation		
Budget Completion		

SPEECH WRITER PLANNER

It is the job of the speech writer to make sure that the candidate says all of the important information in such a way that it will appeal to the audience. It is important to get the candidate's opinion but it is your job to take the ideas and make them strong and important points.

Speech Dates	Speech Length	Main Topics to be Covered
		1. 2. 3.
		1. 2. 3.
		1. 2. 3.

Every speech needs three main sections to make it strong and effective. Follow the outline below to make sure your candidate's speech is the best it can be.

Part 1	Introduction	How will you get the audience's attention? What are the main points that you are going to cover?
Part 2	Body	What detail will you provide about the main points that were mentioned during the introduction? How will you keep the audience's attention?
Part 3	Conclusion	How will you leave the audience remembering your candidate's speech? How will you recap the main points covered in the speech to make sure the audience knows what your candidate believes?

Every good speech is practiced. Have your candidate practice the speech with you (and others in the party) and make changes. Be sure the speech is the right length!

Name:_____

COMMERCIAL DESIGNER PLANNER

It is your job to come up with a commercial that will attract the audience's attention as well as get a strong message across. You will have many factors to consider while making your party's commercial in order to make sure it is effective.

Date to be completed	
Main points to be covered	
Actors or people involved and their roles in the commercial	
Set/Location	
Required props	
Script (you will most likely require more space to complete this section)	

Name:_____

PLANNER

Job during the election: _____

Major responsibilities: _____

_____

_____

_____

_____

Task	Date to be completed	What you will do to make sure the job is completed

Name:_____

CHIEF ELECTORAL OFFICER PLANNER

There is one Chief Electoral Officer in Canada. This person is in charge of Elections Canada and responsible for ensuring the election runs smoothly and that all candidates and parties play by the rules.

Here are some specific examples of the Chief Electoral Officer's responsibilities:

- Ensuring that all parties stay within their budget during an election campaign. Each party may be given a set amount of resources that they may use and the CEO should ensure that parties stay within their "budget".

- Ensuring all parties are leading an honest campaign. This includes monitoring speeches and debates to ensure that parties are not being slanderous.

- Meeting with each party to ensure the rules are being met.

- Making sure that the ridings are equal in number of voters during an election.

- If necessary, voting to break a tie in an election.

- All other responsibilities that make sure the election runs effectively.

As the Chief Electoral Officer, what will you do to ensure that all parties are meeting expectations? Think of what you can do to help the class and teacher make sure that the election is being run properly. For example, you will meet with each party throughout the campaign to ensure the are following the rules. What else will you do?

_____

_____

_____

_____

 **Campaigning**

Name:_____

ACCOUNTANT PLANNER

It takes a lot of money to run a campaign. Some money is provided by the government, some money is given by people involved in the campaign, and a great deal of money is fundraised.

Canadians pay for part of each election through taxes. Each year, the political parties receive about $1.75 for each vote the party received in the previous election. The rest comes from private sources and fundraising.

If a party received five million votes in the last election, how much money would they receive for their campaign?

There are many things to spend money on during a campaign. Consider the following expenses and think about how you would divide a budget of five million dollars.

Item	Cost
Office (furniture, computers)	
Advertising (posters, commercials)	
Transportation (to visit voters)	
Staff (e.g., speech writer) _____ _____ _____ _____	
Other (balloons, stickers)	
Total	**$**

CAMPAIGN POSTER

A campaign poster must catch the eye of the constituency. If people are not interested in looking at the poster, it will not be effective advertising. It must also include all of the necessary information in order to inform voters about the candidate, their party, and their opinions.

An election poster should include the following:

- The candidate's name
- The party for which the candidate is running
- A picture of the candidate
- A slogan
- A logo

Look at the example to help you think of ways to make your poster interesting to look at as well as having all the needed information. Think of what you can do to make your poster attract people's attention. Be sure to plan your poster on a blank page and make sure that you've met all the requirements before you make the final copies.

Be sure to include the following:	Description of your poster
Candidate's name	
Party name	
Logo	
Slogan or phrase	
Picture of the candidate	
Colours	

CANDIDATE INTERVIEW

During an election, the media interview candidates. This is good for parties because it helps to make their points, ideas, and objectives become better known. Interviews also give voters a chance to have their questions answered.

The questions that are asked candidates can serve many purposes. To find out more about the individual candidates, questions may be asked on topics such as:

- Family
- Past careers
- Hobbies
- Personal interests

Questions may be asked to find out a candidate's political stance, such as their position on:

- The environment
- Health care
- Issues concerning the budget

The candidate may also be asked about why they know they are right for the job. These questions will cover topics such as:

- Leadership ability
- Ability to work with people
- Strengths
- Challenges they've faced and how they've overcome them

CANDIDATE INTERVIEW

What would you like to learn about a candidate?

Use this organizer to come up with general ideas about what you would like to learn about a specific candidate, or even all of the candidates.

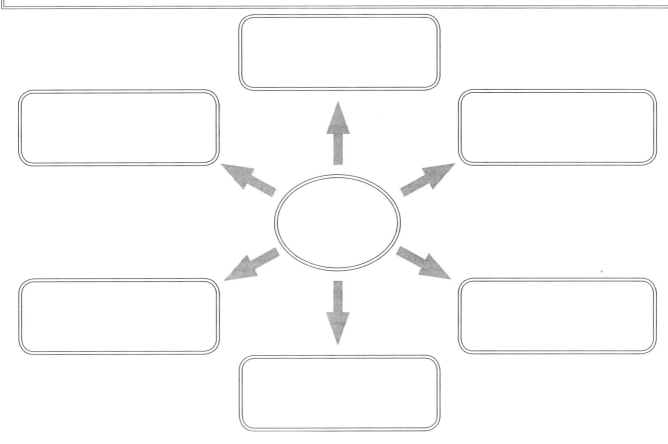

Of all your ideas, what are your most interesting and important questions?

1. _____
   _____

2. _____
   _____

3. _____
   _____

Name:_____

YOUR PARTY'S INTERVIEW QUESTIONS

As a group, look at all of the questions that your party members have. Which questions are the most interesting and important to ask other candidates?

Choose six questions as a group to ask in a candidate interview. If your group is having trouble deciding, look to your party leader to help make any final decisions.

1. _____

_____

2. _____

_____

3. _____

_____

4. _____

_____

5. _____

_____

6. _____

_____

Name:_____

POLLING

The word poll during an election has a variety of meanings. The place where people vote is called the **polling station**. When people go to vote on Election Day, it is often referred to as **going to the polls**.

The word also means to **take a poll**, which is a preliminary vote. It does not count as a vote but it gives the parties and the public some idea of what people are thinking. A poll is a sample to show where people stand. These polls can change from day to day and they may or may not predict the election result.

As a class you will hold one or many polls to find out where your classmates stand at any particular time.

Why do you think the information from a poll is helpful?

_____

_____

_____

_____

_____

What can you do with the information from your classroom poll to help your party out?

_____

_____

_____

_____

During each poll ask yourself what you predict will be the outcome and why.

_____

_____

_____

HOLDING A DEBATE

A debate is a discussion involving opposing viewpoints.

Because a debate involves opposing viewpoints, it can become excited, loud, or even argumentative. It is important that there are specific guidelines set out in order to ensure the debate remains respectful and useful. Use this chart to help you brainstorm ideas about rules that you think are important for a debate to be successful.

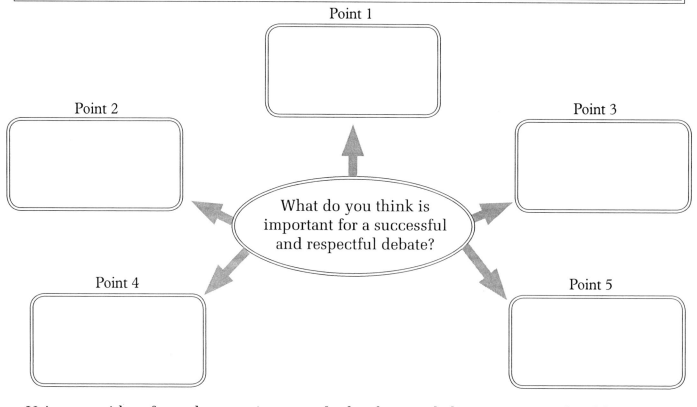

Point 1

Point 2

Point 3

What do you think is important for a successful and respectful debate?

Point 4

Point 5

Using your ideas from above, write a set of rules that you believe everyone should follow during a debate. What are your debate guidelines?

1. _____

   _____

2. _____

   _____

3. _____

   _____

OFFICIAL DEBATE GUIDELINES

1. Your argument should be clearly stated.

2. Your topic should be clearly researched.

3. You should have at least three points that clearly support your position.

4. You are to avoid repetition.

5. Make meaningful, relevant, and constructive points.

6. You are to anticipate the arguments of your opponents.

7. You need to be prepared to counter the arguments of your opponent in a rebuttal.

8. You are to attack the idea, not the person.

9. You should be prepared to rebuild the arguments that your opponent attacks and questions.

10. Your points should be made when no other debaters are speaking and it is your turn to speak.

11. You should argue in a polite and respectful manner.

HOW A DEBATE WORKS

Opening statements – This is a chance for the debater to give their main arguments in an introductory statement. They do not give specific information; they are just to say "this is true because of A and B and C".

Presenting the topics – the debaters present the main arguments for their debate position. Each presenter gives specific details that **prove** A and B and C.

Rebuttal – the debater is to answer the arguments of the other parties' leaders. The debaters must take notes as the other team is presenting their arguments and respond to every argument, using specific information to **disprove** them.

Closing Statement – the debaters present the closing arguments for their position. They are to repeat the main idea and give a summary of the reasons for their positions.

Example Debate Topics:

1. School level

   a) All students should wear school uniforms.

   b) There should be more time for physical education throughout the day.

   c) Teachers should not assign homework.

2. Global level

   a) There should be higher taxes on high emission vehicles.

   b) People who make more money should pay a higher percentage of tax.

   c) Free daycare should be provided for all parents.

WHAT WOULD YOU DEBATE?

Decide upon a topic you would like to debate. Determine the reasons for and against your point using the Pros and Cons chart. Once the chart is complete, use the graphic organizer on the bottom of the page to determine your supporting points for your argument.

Topic: _____

Pros	Cons

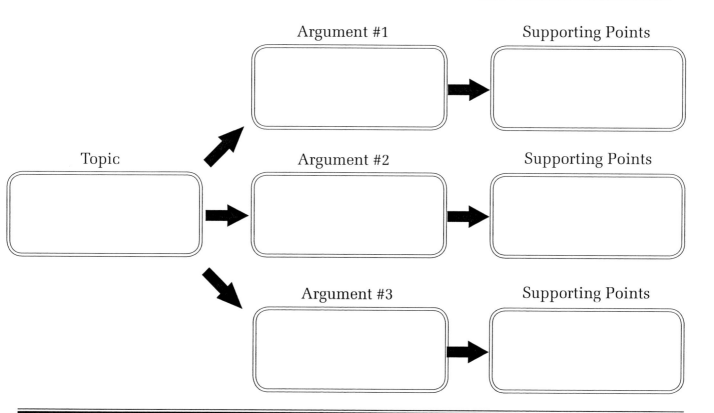

Topic

Argument #1   Supporting Points

Argument #2   Supporting Points

Argument #3   Supporting Points

 Campaigning

Name:_____

CLASSROOM ELECTION DEBATE

Opening Statement: _____

_____

_____

_____

Topics (be detailed):

1. _____

_____

_____

_____

2. _____

_____

_____

_____

3. _____

_____

_____

Predict rebuttals from other parties: _____

_____

_____

_____

Closing statement:_____

_____

_____

_____

_____

TOPICS FOR DEBATE: SOCIAL ISSUES

Every country is faced with a variety of social issues. They may include religion, race, disabilities, or beliefs of any kind. When a government is in power, they do their best to try and solve as many problems that the country faces as they can. This is very hard to do because so many people believe so many different things.

Brainstorm some social issues that you think are important in our country right now.

Social issues faced by Canadians

Choose one specific point from above and research, using the Internet, books, pamphlets and articles, how a political party is currently involved with this issue.
Where do they stand?

_____

_____

_____

_____

_____

What changes do they want to make?

_____

_____

_____

_____

TOPICS FOR DEBATE: EDUCATION

Education is primarily the provincial government's jurisdiction, although the federal government provides some direction in terms of financial support and some policy-making. The provinces decide on the curriculum that is taught and the money that will be spent on education each year.

In the space below, research some beliefs of a variety of your province's political parties. Include information on any policy about education that they support.

Party	Policy or Point of View

Think about the information you found about the above parties and their policies on education. What did you learn?

_____

_____

_____

_____

Do you agree or disagree with any of the above ideas? Why or why not?

_____

_____

_____

_____

TOPICS FOR DEBATE: ENVIRONMENT

The environment is a very popular issue at the moment. Both the provincial and federal governments are greatly involved in developing policies to help protect the environment. The parties often do not agree on how they can best protect the environment while not damaging the economy.

Use the space below to find out different parties stances on what can be done to help our environment.

Party	Environmental Policies

Thinking about the information above, what have you learned about the environment and our country's environmental policies?

_____

_____

_____

Which ideas or policies do you most agree with? Why?

_____

_____

_____

Name:_____

TOPICS FOR DEBATE: EMPLOYMENT

All levels of government are responsible for their jurisdiction's employment rate to a certain extent. Ideally a government would like every person who is of working age and not in school to have a job. The government develops policies to try and make that happen. We are told how well this has been achieved by the unemployment rate, which tells us what percentage of people is unemployed at the time.

Use the space below to research how different parties attempt to lower the unemployment rate.

Party	Tactic to Reduce Unemployment

What have you learned about your country's policies on unemployment?

_____

_____

_____

Which ideas or policies do you most agree with? Why?

_____

_____

_____

_____

Name:_____

TOPICS FOR DEBATE: HEALTH CARE

Canada spends a lot of time and resources making sure that it is providing a strong health care system for its inhabitants. All the parties feel there are different ways to provide the highest standard of health care. Every time someone is sick they need to see a doctor or go to the hospital and the government must make sure that the necessary resources are there to help them.

Using the space below, find out how different parties feel that the issue of proper health care should be addressed.

Party	Stance on Health Care

What have you learned about your country's policies on health care?

_____

_____

_____

Which ideas or policies do you most agree with? Why?

_____

_____

_____

TOPICS FOR DEBATE: YOUR SCHOOL

Your school, just like your country, faces many challenges every day. There are rules put into place to try and make sure that every student has a safe, educational, and happy experience at school. Even with these rules and guidelines, we sometimes feel that we are not happy or safe or learning what we think we should be.

Think about your school experience. Write down some points that make you feel unhappy, unsafe, or that you are not effectively learning. Or think about ways your school could be improved.

- _____
  _____

- _____
  _____

- _____
  _____

- _____
  _____

- _____
  _____

What rule or policy might you think of that could help improve one of the points above? How?

_____
_____
_____
_____

Who would be involved in implementing your new "policy"? A student, teacher, or the principal?

_____

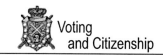
Voting and Citizenship

Goal: Students will learn that voting is both a right and responsibility along with other rights and responsibilities of citizenship. They will also learn the process of voting that occurs on election day. At this point, it is getting close to election time and it's important for the students to understand what it means to vote in Canada. It is something that everyone is the country has worked hard for and it's important to stress that it is not something that we should take lightly.

The Right to Vote and Canadian Citizenship: *(page 69)*
Read this page as a class and highlight any points that the students find particularly interesting.

Extension: Explore groups that had to fight to get the right to vote in Canada.

You Are a Citizen of Your School: *(page 70)*
The teacher may wish to brainstorm some ideas as a class as to what it means to be a citizen of the country and of the school.

The students are then to use the Venn Diagram to compare the school and the country. Topics that just apply to the school go in the school section, topics that just apply to the country go in the country section, and topics that apply to both go in the middle section.

Your Rights and Responsibilities As a Canadian: *(page 71)*
Students are to make a list of what they feel their rights and responsibilities are as a citizen of Canada. Teachers may prompt with questions such as:
    What are you allowed to do every day?
    What places do you go every day?
    What is put in place to make you feel safe as a Canadian citizen?

The Rights and Responsibilities of All Canadians: *(page 72)*
The teacher should encourage each student to compare their "What Are Your Rights and Responsibilities" list to the one given on this page. Teacher questions might include:
    What is similar on the lists?
    What is different?
    Why did you write down what you did?
    Do you think it should be included? Why or why not?

Have the students use the bottom of the page to compare how the school and the country are alike.

Citizen Certificate: *(page 73)*
Once each student has completed the citizenship, rights, and responsibilities section they may receive a certificate to show that they are a citizen of the school. The teacher may wish to have a ceremony to hand out the certificates and explain that each student now has the right and responsibility to vote responsibly in their class election.

Your Classroom Ridings – A Coordinate Mapping Activity: *(page 74)*
Explain to the students what a riding is (see glossary if needed). Explain that each riding should contain a similar number of people and people should vote in a location that is convenient for everyone in that riding.

Each classroom should have two or more ridings. The students should start off by drawing a picture of the classroom using the grid and lines to show where each riding boundary would be. The students should use coordinates to explain where the riding boundaries go.

The teacher should also have their own map to show ridings ready for use at election time.

What Happens After the Election: *(page 75)*
The teacher should have the students read through this sheet to help them interpret the final election results.

Ballot Templates: *(page 76)*
The teacher should review this sheet with their students to ensure they understand how a ballot should be properly filled out. The importance of this should be stressed because in real life a vote will not count if it is not done properly. It will help the students to be familiar with the ballot before the election takes place.

The Campaign Review: *(page 77)*
Just prior to the election, a review exercise works well. Read through the campaign process as a class and ask the students to think about each of the parties and how well they followed the process. Encourage students to answer questions thoroughly and with thought. You may wish to include peer or self-assessment at this time.

Holding the Election

During the election, it is important to set the classroom up to mimic an actual election. Ideally there should be more than one polling station where the students go to cast their vote. Students can be divided up into separate groups based on where they live, alphabetical order, where they sit in the class or any other way that separates them into groups.

The classroom should be set up so that each student knows their riding and the location of the polling station. The teacher may wish to tell students that they may vote at any time during the day or they may have the students vote during a set period.

Use the ballot templates and put enough at each polling station for each student.

Once the students have voted, it is the teacher's responsibility to tally the votes. The results should be read after the polls have closed.

** It is important that teachers remind their students before they vote that they are not voting as a party member. They should vote for the candidate and party they feel would do the best job in government, based on their campaign.

The polling stations should be set up so that they are apart from one another and each one should have a three-sided cardboard cover surrounding it so that other students cannot see while one is voting. There should be pencils and ballots at each station. The teacher may wish to hand the ballots out or appoint students to do the job. There should also be a cardboard box with a slit in it at each station. This is where the students are to put their filled out ballots. The polling stations should be built by the teacher or this could be a job for the CEO to ensure fair polling stations.

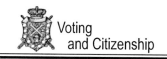

Diagram of sample classroom set up for the election.

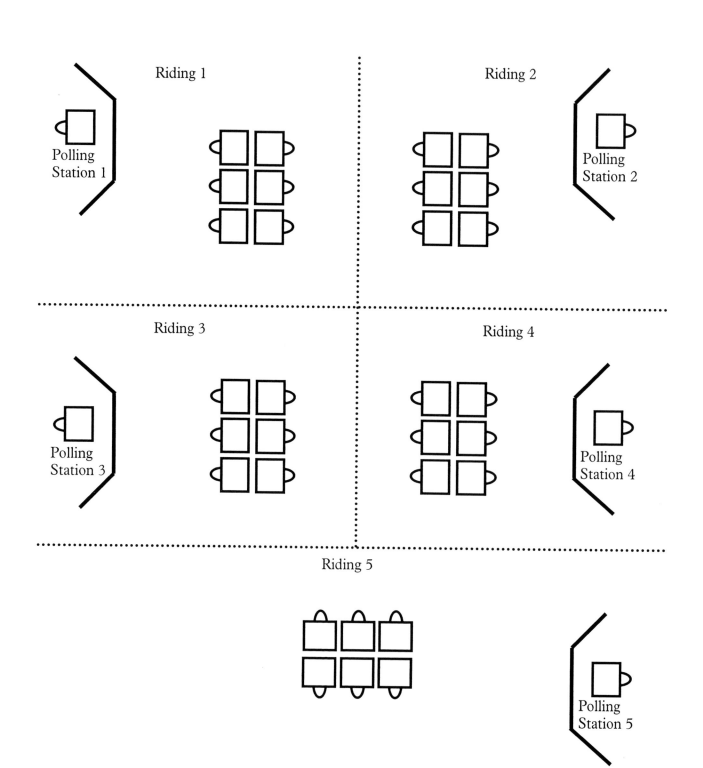

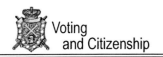
THE RIGHT TO VOTE AND CANADIAN CITIZENSHIP

To vote in an election in Canada you must be 18 or older and you must be a Canadian citizen.

Any Canadian citizen who is 18 has the right to vote in Canada, but it was not always this way. For example:

- It was not until 1940 that women over the age of 21 gained the right to vote in federal elections in Canada.

- In 1960 all ethnic groups were allowed to vote in Canada.

- In 1982 the Canadian Charter of Rights and Freedoms made it official that all Canadian citizens over the age of 18 were allowed to vote in Canada.

This means that there are over 22 million people in Canada who have the right to vote.

A citizen is someone who is part of a community, so in order to be a Canadian citizen you must be part of Canada. A citizen has all the rights and freedoms that allow them to take part in Canada's society.

You can become a Canadian citizen in one of two ways: be born in Canada or move to Canada and, over time, meet all of the necessary requirements.

The requirements to become a Canadian citizen are as follows:

- You must live in Canada for a minimum of three years

- You must be able to speak one of Canada's national languages, French or English

- You must also show that you have knowledge of Canadian laws and customs

As a citizen of Canada you have many benefits but it is also important to be a positive member of your community, whether it's your school, city, or country. What ways can you be a strong Canadian citizen?

_____

_____

_____

_____

YOU ARE A CITIZEN OF YOUR SCHOOL

If a citizen is a member of a community then you are also a citizen of your school or your classroom. As a citizen of your school, you have many rights and responsibilities and you are also expected to play a role in making your school or community a success. You are expected to show respect and follow the laws and rules set out by the community of which you are a citizen.

Think of all the ways that citizenship of a school and a country is the same. Think of how they are different. Use this Venn diagram below to show your conclusions.

How is being a citizen of your school like being a citizen of your country?
What are your rights and responsibilities as a Canadian?

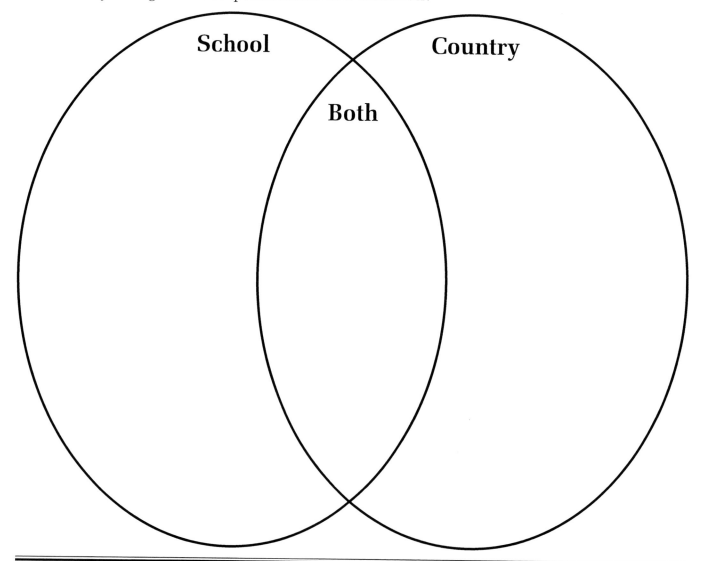

YOUR RIGHTS AND RESPONSIBILITIES AS A CANADIAN

To answer this, think about all the things you might do in a day: go to school, go shopping, go to church, go on a trip, learn French.

What things do you have the right to do, whether it's in school, at home, or somewhere else? A right is a thing that you are guaranteed to have.

Name three rights you have in Canada:

* _____

_____

* _____

_____

* _____

_____

You also have responsibilities to your school and to your country. What are your responsibilities when you're at school or out in your community? A responsibility is a thing you are expected to do to be a contributing member of Canadian society.

Name three responsibilities you have in Canada:

* _____

_____

* _____

_____

* _____

_____

THE RIGHTS AND RESPONSIBILITIES OF ALL CANADIANS

Compare the list you made to these official lists.

The Rights of a Canadian Citizen:

- A citizen has the right to equal treatment before the laws of Canada

- A citizen has the right to leave and re-enter Canada

- A citizen has the right to their own personal beliefs

- A citizen has the right to speak French or English

- A citizen has the right to vote

- A citizen has the right to a lawyer if and when needed

- A citizen has the right to be presumed innocent until proven guilty

The Responsibilities of a Canadian Citizen:

- A citizen must follow the rules laid out by Canadian laws

- A citizen has the responsibility to vote during an election

- A citizen is not to interfere with other Canadians' rights

- A citizen should appreciate and preserve the multiculturalism in Canada

How do the rights and responsibilities of Canada compare to the rights and responsibilities at your school? Be sure to explain your answer.

_____

_____

_____

_____

_____

_____

CITIZEN CERTIFICATE

_____
Name

is officially a citizen of

_____ *School*

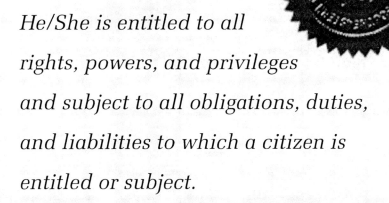

He/She is entitled to all

rights, powers, and privileges

and subject to all obligations, duties,

and liabilities to which a citizen is

entitled or subject.

_____
Date

_____
Teacher's Signature

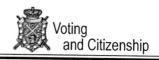
YOUR CLASSROOM RIDINGS

Your class is going to be divided up into separate ridings. This is to help mimic a true government election. Ridings are determined by location and the number of people in each location. This is to try and make every vote equal.

Using coordinates, draw a detailed map of your classroom and show how you would divide the students up to make sure that ridings are equal and the locations make sense.

(Your teacher will assign the final ridings and poll station locations for your election day.)

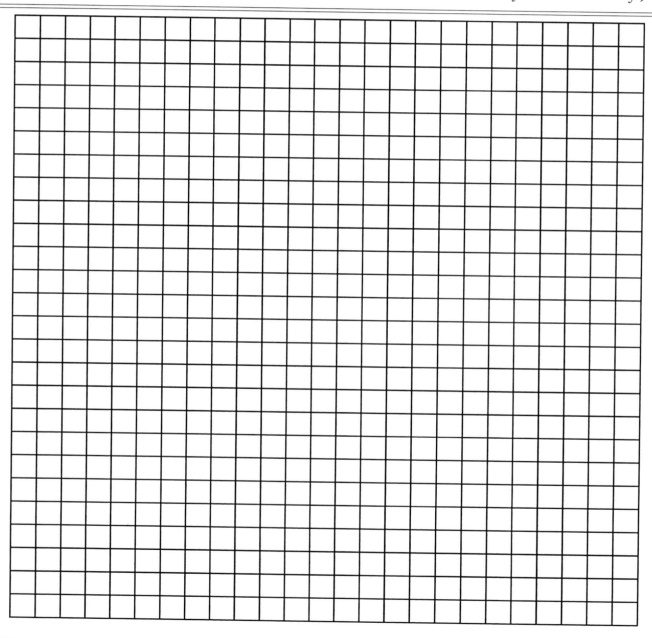

WHAT HAPPENS AFTER THE ELECTION?

When a candidate wins an election they can have either a majority or minority government. A majority government is when a party wins more than half of the ridings in an election. A minority government is when a party wins the most seats (which are determined by riding) but they do not win more than half.

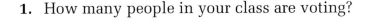

Because a classroom is much smaller than a federal election, we will use votes instead of ridings or seats.

1. How many people in your class are voting?

   _____

2. How many votes would a candidate need to win the majority of votes? Remember, a majority means more than half. Show this number as a fraction. For example, if there are 25 students in your class, the candidate would need 13 to win the majority of the votes. The fraction would be 13/25.)

   _____

3. Show two different ways that the votes in the class could be divided up so that there is a winner of the election but they do not have the minority of the votes.

   _____

4. What percentage of votes does a candidate need to win the election?

   _____

5. What percentage does a candidate need to win the election with the majority of votes?

   _____

6. How could you show the percentages in questions 4 and 5 as a decimal?

   _____

BALLOT TEMPLATES

On the day of the election you will be given a **ballot**. This is the piece of paper you use to tell the country who you would like to win the election. When the ballot is filled out it is very important that it is done properly. The only person who should see the ballot is the one casting the vote. When they mark in their chosen candidate they must make a clear mark with the writing implement given. If the mark is not clear, the ballot may be considered a **spoiled ballot**, and the vote will not count.

_____Classroom Election

	NAME:	PARTY:
○	NAME:	PARTY:
○	NAME:	PARTY:
○	NAME:	PARTY:
○	NAME:	PARTY:

_____Classroom Election

	NAME:	PARTY:
○	NAME:	PARTY:
○	NAME:	PARTY:
○	NAME:	PARTY:
○	NAME:	PARTY:

THE CAMPAIGN REVIEW

Look over your Election Checklist.

In detail, explain how your party properly participated in each step of the election process. Be sure to include how successful your party was at each step and why.

1. Your leader candidates (who ran for party leader?)

_____

_____

_____

2. Party nomination (how did your party decide upon a winner?)

_____

_____

_____

3. Your election campaign (what went well, what did not?)

_____

_____

_____

4. Election day

_____

_____

_____

5. After the election

_____

_____

Mock Parliament

Goal: Students will learn the basic processes our government goes through to make laws and changes in our country.

Parliamentary Procedures: *(page 80)*
This page is intended as background information to help students understand how laws and bills are made in Canada.

The Roles of Members of Parliament: *(page 81)*
The students should understand what each role in parliament is and why they are needed. The roles are already decided by the election. Different ministers are appointed by the party leader (e.g., Minister of the Environment, Transportation, Industry, etc.), although the teacher may want to appoint the Speaker of the House to ensure it is a student who will be confident in the position. The questions on the bottom of the page are to encourage students to start thinking about how they will play their roles.

Mock Parliament Procedures: *(page 82)*
The classroom parliament can mimic real parliament by following these steps.

What Changes Would You Make?: *(page 83)*
This sheet is intended to get students thinking about what motions they will bring up during mock parliament.

Making a Difference: *(page 84)*
This sheet may help students decide upon topics for parliament or encourage them to take a stand on an issue outside of the mock parliament sessions.

Extension: A student can take the making a difference questions and form a plan on their chosen issue and think of ways that they could actually implement their plan.

Passing a Bill: *(page 85)*
The teacher should lead the students through the steps that are outlined but it is not suggested that this process be used in the classroom.

Passing a Bill in Your Classroom: *(page 86)*
Students should use this page to prepare their proposed law which can then be brought to the mock parliament and it can be brought forward during the New Business segment.

Calling an Election: *(page 87)*
If time permits, the teacher may want to lead the class through the election process again at a certain point in the year. This would give a new student the chance to be the Prime Minister. The teacher may also wish to use this sheet in a hypothetical manner. This will help students to understand why an election might be called.

Classroom Parliament Set-up

The classroom should be set up in such a way that it mimics the House of Commons. The Speaker should be in a chair at the front of the class to perform their role.

The governing party should be to one side of the Speaker and the other parties on the other side of the speaker, with the Leader of the Opposition in the front.

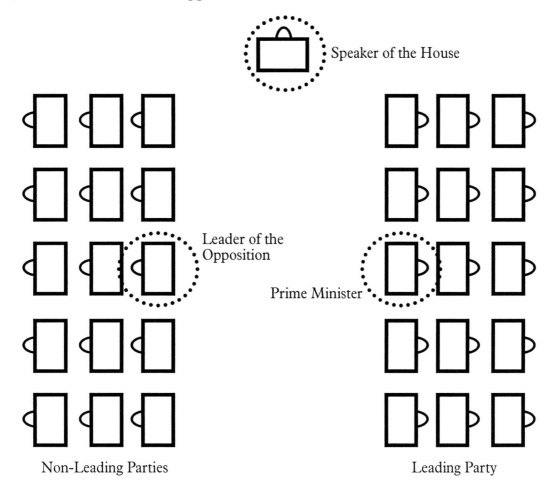

Once the election has been held and each position has been determined, the class can decide on important points that should be discussed. They can choose items that are relevant to the classroom, school, or country.

Depending on the law or bill that the class would like to pass, they can decide to make them official class "laws".

PARLIAMENTARY PROCEDURES

Before governments can make changes, they must first decide what changes are needed. All of the members of the parties get together and hold a party caucus. This is when they have a chance to decide what approaches they will take to make sure their ideas are put into practice.

Question Period begins later on in the day. This is the time for parties to interact with each other and discuss issues as a large group. Bills (ideas) may be introduced at this point and these bills may eventually become new Canadian laws.

All questions asked during Question Period must be directed to the Speaker of the House. This is to help keep things running smoothly and to help to make sure that questions stay as positive as possible. Members of Parliament (MPs) must make sure they ask clear, brief questions that are directed to a specific person.

When a government is elected, the Prime Minister must choose people to become Cabinet Ministers. These are the people who are in charge of specific areas of the government (for example, the Minister of Health or the Minister of the Environment).

The Cabinet is the group of people who make most of the new and important decisions. This is why it is important to make informed decisions when voting to ensure that the people in charge will most likely make decisions you agree with.

The Official Opposition is all Members of Parliament of all the parties that did not win the election. They are still in parliament and share opposing views to the governing party to ensure that all sides of the argument have been explored.

Questions:

Why is it important for there to be an opposition?

Why should there be specific ministers?

Challenge: Compare a democracy to a dictatorship.

THE ROLES OF MEMBERS OF PARLIAMENT

Cabinet Minister – a person who plays a special role in the cabinet. He or she is appointed by the Prime Minister to look after a specific ministry. The Ministries include Health, Environment, Social Services, Natural Resources, and Fisheries. Ministers are individuals who usually have some expertise in that area.

Official Opposition – this is all the elected MPs who belong to the party that received the second greatest number of votes in the election. People in the official opposition are often given a shadow role and it is their job to keep track of the Cabinet Ministers in the governing party. They are the ones who will bring up points to argue with the Cabinet Minister if they do not agree with what is being said.

Prime Minister – the person who is the leader of the governing party or party with the most seats in the House of Commons. It is the Prime Minister's job to appoint Cabinet Ministers for the various ministries.

Speaker of the House – an elected member of the government who is in charge of ensuring that parliamentary rules and procedures are followed while the House of Commons is in session.

1. Now the election is over, which role will you play in your class's Parliament? Why?

   _____

   _____

   _____

2. What can you do to prepare for that role?

   _____

   _____

MOCK PARLIAMENT PROCEDURES

Each meeting of parliament should include the following:

Step 1 – The meeting is called to order by the Speaker of the House who is responsible for ensuring that everyone is ready to start to proceedings.

Step 2 – The Speaker of the House reads the notes from the last meeting. This will help refresh everyone's memories as to what are the main issues at the moment.

Step 3 – Any committees that have been formed to tackle a particular issue are to report on any progress that is made. Any Members of Parliament may form a committee if they feel that there is an issue that they would like to pursue.

Step 4 – New Business should be brought forth. Any Member of Parliament may choose to bring up a new issue that they believe needs to be addressed and where they would like to see changes be made. Once the issue has been put forward there must be another Member of Parliament who is willing to second the motion or stand by it. If the motion gets seconded then the topic is up for discussion in parliament. When someone is interested in speaking they must raise their hand. The Speaker writes down individual names in order and informs them when it's their turn to speak.

After discussion, parliament may vote on the issue to see if it will be passed.

Step 5 – The Speaker of the House will adjourn or end the meeting.

WHAT CHANGES WOULD YOU MAKE?

When you think about your school, community, or country, do you ever wish things were a little different? Would you prefer they served a different hot lunch at school? Or would you like to see stricter rules about unemployment?

Use the chart below to think of what changes you would make at the various levels of government. Maybe you can make a difference.

School	Community	Province	Country

MAKING A DIFFERENCE

Students all across the country take action to make real changes in our world. When a student feels strongly about a topic they are sometimes inclined to see how they can make a difference. It often starts off small but can lead to much larger things. It could be raising money to save an endangered species, or raising money for a new community centre. It could also be starting a petition to help stop a bill from being passed and made into law in parliament.

If you decided to take on an issue you feel strongly about, whether at the school or country level, what would it be?

_____

_____

_____

_____

Why do you feel strongly about this issue?

_____

_____

_____

_____

What steps could you take, as a student, to help this cause?

_____

_____

_____

_____

PASSING A BILL

When a bill is passed it becomes a law. Because a law is a very big decision, it means that passing a bill is a fairly in-depth process so that not just anything can become a law.

It is very important to have rules and laws so that all citizens of our country can feel safe and the country can operate effectively.

A party decides what they believe should be a law

The House of Commons may pass the bill with the changes

The bill is studied again by the Senate and further changes may be suggested

In the House of Commons a Cabinet Member presents the bill

Some changes may be made to the bill

The Governor General signs the bill

While the House of Commons is in session, the bill is debated

A group of MPs get together to study the bill

The bill is now a law and it can be enforced

PASSING A BILL IN YOUR CLASSROOM

In the previous pages you explored changes you might make to your school, community, province, or country. Take one of those changes and turn it into a bill to present in parliament. In order for it to be a bill, you need to state what the new law would be and the reasons for it.

1. Make one of your proposed changes into a statement that could be enforced as a law. For example, "Students should be allowed to wear hats in the hallways of their school."

   Statement: _____

   _____

   _____

2. Explain the potential new law. For example, "Hats in the hallway do not interfere with student learning. The do not hurt anyone physically or emotionally. Students may more easily loose their hats if they are not on their heads."

   Explanation: _____

   _____

   _____

   _____

   _____

   _____

   _____

   _____

Now that you have a bill, it can be presented in your class's House of Commons. Maybe you can make a new law for your classroom that all students must follow!

CALLING AN ELECTION

How do we know it's time to have an election? It is the Prime Minister's job to call an election or to state when an election will be held.

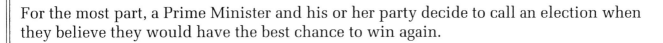

An election must happen at least once every five years but they usually happen more often than that. A Prime Minister may also call an election when he or she can't get enough MPs to vote yes for an important question in the House of Commons. When the Prime Minister can't get enough yes votes, this is called losing "a vote of confidence". The government has failed, and an election must be called. This does not happen often.

For the most part, a Prime Minister and his or her party decide to call an election when they believe they would have the best chance to win again.

When an election is called, there must be at least 36 days for all the parties to campaign, but most of the time, everyone is given more time than that to prepare. The election must be held on a Monday.

When do you think is a good time for your class to call an election?

_____

_____

_____

What reasons do you have for your answer?

_____

_____

_____

_____

_____

_____

Conclusion

Goal: To wrap up the election experience and assess students' thinking.

Guest Speaker:
A guest speaker can be called in at any time. This will need to be agreed upon between the teacher and the guest speaker. The guest speaker may be a local politician or perhaps someone who is a retired politician. The teacher may contact a current politician's office.

As the teacher, it is important to explain to the guest that you are currently running an election in your classroom. They should be asked to highlight their election and campaign experiences.

The teacher should lead the class in a discussion before the guest speaker comes to identify areas where students might have questions and share this information with your guest <u>prior</u> to their visit. It is important for the teacher to share information about the guest speaker to give students an idea of whom they will be meeting. Read over the points on the guest Speaker Worksheet page to start the brainstorming process of what the students wish to know.

Guest Speaker Worksheet: *(page 89)*
It is a good idea to review students' questions before the guest comes and encourage students to choose one of their questions to prepare to ask the guest, or be assigned one of their questions to ask the guest.

It will be helpful to the guest speaker to provide him/her with your students' questions beforehand as this will assist them in planning their presentation.

Classroom Election Research Project : *(page 90)*
These topics can be used as an extension or enrichment.

Assessments and Answer Key: *(pages 92-96)*
Two types of assessments are included: short answer and open response essay questions. Answers are provided for Assessment #1 but answers will vary for Assessment #2.

GUEST SPEAKER

Having a guest speaker come into your class can help you to learn more about running a successful campaign. This gives you an opportunity to find out more about elections. Ask yourself if a career in politics for you!

You may wish to ask a guest speaker questions about:

- How to have a successful election campaign
- Challenges they've faced
- What they find most difficult
- Time spent on the election or the job itself
- How an election effects family life
- Some of the best or most exciting things they've experienced

What other things would you like to know about elections and government?

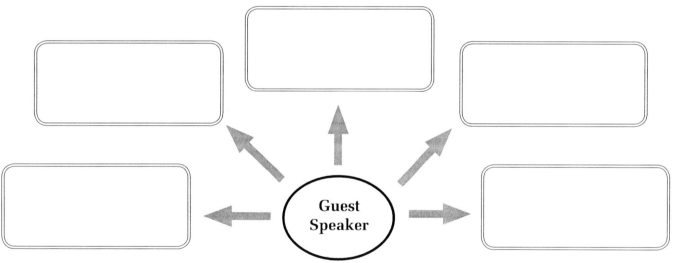

Use the ideas in this graphic organizer to write three good questions for the guest speaker.

1. _____

_____

2. _____

_____

3. _____

_____

CLASSROOM ELECTION RESEARCH PROJECT

Choose one of the following challenges:

1. Research a Canadian political leader. Explain their leadership background and the changes that they have made to Canada. Do you believe they played an important role? Why or why not?

2. Write a letter to a Member of Parliament stating your opinion on a current policy or law with which you don't agree. Be sure to research the topic closely to ensure that all your points are correct.

3. Choose a bill that has been passed by the House of Commons. Follow that bill from when it was first introduced until it was passed. Include information about all of the steps including the time it took.

4. If you were a Cabinet Minister, which ministry would you be responsible for? How would you make a difference?

5. Choose a political party and research the changes that have occurred to that party. What differences have they made to our country?

6. Research the history of women in government. Include issues such as the first female MP, the first female Prime Minister, and when women gained the right to vote.

7. In detail, explain the steps that an individual must take to become a Canadian citizen. Why is this important?

8. Choose a major issue that Canada is facing today. Explain the issue and what actions the Canadian government is taking. What is your opinion on Canada's approach to this issue?

RESEARCH PROJECT ORGANIZER

Use this organizer to keep track of important resources and information you've found to help you with your project.

Chosen Topic:

Important Web Sites:

Other Resources:

Key Points:

_____

_____

_____

_____

_____

_____

Introductory Statement:

Concluding Statement:

CLASSROOM ELECTION TEST #1

1. It is the Governor General's job to call an election for the country?   **True** or **False**

2. Which of the following parties believes that the environment is the most important issue, and without a healthy environment, we cannot have a healthy economy?

    a) The Liberal Party

    b) The Conservative Party

    c) The Green Party

    d) The New Democratic Party

3. When a bill is passed by the House of Commons, what does it become? Why is this important?

    _____

    _____

    _____

    _____

4. Name three qualities that you believe a strong government leader should have. Why are these qualities important?

    a) _____

    _____

    b) _____

    _____

    c) _____

    _____

CLASSROOM ELECTION TEST #1 CONT'D

5. What does it mean to be a Cabinet Minister?

_____

_____

_____

6. **a)** Who can vote in Canada?

_____

b) Has it always been this way?

_____

_____

7. Name <u>two</u> things that each of the following levels of government are responsible for:

Municipal – _____

_____

Provincial – _____

_____

Federal – _____

_____

_____

Name:_____

CLASSROOM ELECTION TEST #2

Answer three of the following essay questions. Be sure to include an introduction, body, and conclusion, as well as details to back up what you believe.

1. If you were running to be a Member of Parliament, what would be the main issues covered in your platform?

_____

_____

_____

_____

_____

2. Who do you believe is a strong Canadian leader (they do not have to be a government leader)? Why do you think they are such a strong leader?

_____

_____

_____

_____

_____

3. If you were to belong to a Canadian political party, which one would it be and why?

_____

_____

_____

_____

_____

CLASSROOM ELECTION TEST #2 CONT'D

4. As a voter in an election, what must you do to inform yourself to know whom to vote for? How can you do this?

_____

_____

_____

_____

_____

5. If you had a meeting with your Member of Parliament, what questions would you ask him or her? Why would you ask those questions?

_____

_____

_____

_____

_____

6. If you could pass any bill in Parliament, what would it be? Remember to explain your reasoning.

_____

_____

_____

_____

_____

Answer Key

Test #1: *(page 92)*

1. False – it is the Prime Minister's job to call an election for the country.

2. **c)** The Green Party

3. A bill becomes a law when the House of Commons passes it. This is important because we need to help elect people who will make good laws for our country. Laws are important to help keep us safe and protected and to tell us what is expected.

4. Answers may vary.
   Examples include: dedication, being able to work as a team, good ideas, commitment, respected, strong, standing up for what they believe, etc.

5. A Cabinet Minister – an MP who has been appointed by the Prime Minister to be responsible for a specific area of the government (e.g., Environment).

6. **a)** Anyone who is over the age of 18 and a citizen of Canada may vote.
   b) No, there were times when women, aboriginal people, disabled people, and others could not vote.

7. Municipal – Snow removal, garbage removal, libraries, etc.
   Provincial – Education, road and highway construction, etc.
   Federal – Environment, immigration, etc.

Test #2: *(page 94)*
Answers may vary.